© 2024 by FAISAL JAMIL. All rights reserved.

Title: "Sales Symphony: The Art and Science of Strategic Selling"

This book, along with its contents encompassing text, illustrations, images, diagrams, and other creative elements, is the exclusive property of FAISAL JAMIL and is safeguarded by copyright law.

FAISAL JAMIL asserts full ownership and retains all rights to this book. No part of this publication may be reproduced, distributed, or transmitted in any form or by any means, such as photocopying, recording, or electronic methods, without prior written consent from the copyright holder. Brief quotations in critical reviews and certain noncommercial uses permitted by copyright law are exceptions.

This copyright notice applies to all editions, formats, and translations of the book, whether in print, digital, or any other medium or technology existing now or developed in the future. Unauthorized use or infringement may result in legal action and pursuit of remedies under applicable copyright laws.

While efforts have been made to ensure accuracy and reliability, FAISAL JAMIL does not guarantee the completeness or suitability of the information. Readers are responsible for evaluating and using the content judiciously.

FAISAL JAMIL reserves the right to make changes, updates, or corrections to the book without prior notice. Inclusion of third-party materials or references does not imply endorsement or affiliation unless used under fair use principles or with proper permissions and attributions.

For permissions, inquiries, or requests regarding the book's use, please contact FAISAL JAMIL through official channels listed on their Amazon author page or provided email address.

This comprehensive copyright notice serves to protect FAISAL JAMIL'S intellectual property rights, maintain content control, and inform users about associated restrictions and permissions.

Warm regards,

FAISAL JAMIL

For your feedback and reviews:

https://www.amazon.com/author/faisal.jamil

Email: faisaljamilauthor@gmail.com

About the author

Certainly! Faisal Jamil is a multifaceted individual with a diverse set of skills and experiences. With a strong foundation in computer knowledge since childhood, he has developed a deep understanding of technology that informs his work as a content writer. Faisal also possesses digital skills, which further enhance his abilities in various digital platforms and technologies.

Beyond his professional endeavors, Faisal Jamil has also excelled in the martial arts, particularly Shotokan Karate, where he achieved the prestigious rank of first Dan black belt. This achievement speaks to his dedication, discipline, and commitment to personal growth and mastery.

In his professional life, Faisal Jamil has carved out a successful career in sales management within the Fast Moving Consumer Goods (FMCG) sector. His roles in various FMCG companies have honed his skills in strategic planning, team leadership, and business development. Faisal's ability to drive sales and achieve targets has been instrumental in his career progression, showcasing his talent for identifying opportunities and delivering results.

Faisal Jamil is also deeply interested in business investment strategies, planning, and execution. His understanding of these areas has been key to his success in the business world, allowing him to make informed decisions and implement effective strategies. His ability to navigate the complexities of investment planning and execution has set him apart as a strategic thinker and a valuable asset in any business endeavor.

Overall, Faisal Jamil is a dynamic individual who combines his passion for technology, martial arts, sales management, digital skills, and business investment strategies to achieve success in diverse fields. His journey is a testament to his versatility, resilience, and continuous pursuit of excellence.

Yours Sincerely

FAISAL JAMIL

For your feedback and reviews:

https://www.amazon.com/author/faisal.jamil

Email: faisaljamilauthor@gmail.com

SALES SYMPHONY
THE ART AND SCIENCE OF
STRATEGIC SELLING

Table of Content

Preface

Chapter 1: The Foundation of Sales Strategy

Chapter 2: Market Analysis and Competitive Intelligence

Chapter 3: Building a Strong Sales Team

Chapter 4: Developing a Sales Plan

Chapter 5: Crafting a Compelling Value Proposition

Chapter 6: Sales Process Optimization

Chapter 7: Effective Sales Techniques

Chapter 8: Sales Metrics and Performance Tracking

Chapter 9: Sales Strategy in the Digital Age

Chapter 10: Global Sales Strategies

Chapter 11: Crisis Management and Contingency Planning

Chapter 12: Ethical Selling Practices

Conclusion: The Future of Sales Strategy

Preface:

Welcome to "Sales Symphony: The Art and Science of Strategic Selling." This book is designed to be your comprehensive guide to mastering the strategic aspects of selling, combining the art of building relationships with the science of data-driven decision-making.

In today's fast-paced and competitive business environment, successful selling requires more than just charisma and persuasion. It requires a strategic approach that is grounded in a deep understanding of customer needs, market dynamics, and effective sales techniques.

"Sales Symphony" is divided into three main sections:

1: Understanding the Sales Process: This section lays the foundation for effective selling by exploring the key stages of the sales process, from prospecting to closing deals. You'll learn how to identify potential customers, qualify leads, and present solutions that meet their needs.

2: Strategic Selling Techniques: Here, you'll discover advanced selling techniques that will help you differentiate yourself from competitors, overcome objections, and close deals more effectively. You'll also learn how to leverage technology and data analytics to improve your sales performance.

3: Building Long-Term Relationships: The final section of the book focuses on building long-term relationships with customers. You'll learn how to cultivate trust, provide exceptional customer service, and create loyalty that extends beyond the initial sale.

Throughout the book, you'll find practical tips, real-world examples, and actionable strategies that you can apply immediately to improve your sales performance. Whether you're a seasoned sales professional or new to the field, "Sales Symphony" will equip you with the tools and knowledge you need to succeed in today's competitive sales landscape.

Thank you for choosing "Sales Symphony." We hope this book serves as a valuable resource on your journey to mastering the art and science of strategic selling.

Chapter 1: The Foundation of Sales Strategy

A: Understanding the Sales Process

The sales process is a systematic approach to selling a product or service. It involves a series of steps that a salesperson takes to identify, qualify, and close a sale. Understanding this process is crucial for developing an effective sales strategy.

1: Prospecting:

This is the first step in the sales process, where the salesperson identifies potential customers or leads. This can be done through various methods such as cold calling, networking, or using online tools.

Prospecting is a critical step in the sales process that sets the foundation for building a successful customer base. Here's a detailed explanation of prospecting:

a: Definition: Prospecting is the process of identifying and qualifying potential customers or leads who may have an interest in the products or services offered by a business. It involves gathering information about individuals or organizations that fit the criteria of an ideal customer.

b: Methods of Prospecting:

1: Cold Calling: This involves reaching out to potential customers via phone without any prior contact. It requires a salesperson to introduce themselves, their company, and the products or services they offer.

2: Networking: Networking involves building relationships with individuals or businesses that may lead to potential sales opportunities. This can be done through attending industry events, joining professional organizations, or using social media platforms.

3: Online Tools: There are various online tools and platforms available that can help salespeople identify potential leads, such as CRM software, social media platforms, and lead generation websites.

4: Referrals: Existing customers or contacts can provide valuable referrals to potential leads who may be interested in the products or services offered.

c: Qualifying Leads: Once potential leads are identified, they need to be qualified to ensure they meet the criteria of an ideal customer. This may involve gathering information about their needs, budget, timeline, and decision-making process.

d: Building Relationships: Prospecting is not just about finding new leads but also about building relationships with them. Salespeople should focus on establishing trust and credibility with potential customers to increase the likelihood of a successful sale.

e: Tracking and Follow-Up: It's important for salespeople to track their prospecting activities and follow up with leads in a timely manner. This may involve using a CRM system to manage leads and schedule follow-up calls or meetings.

f: Continuous Improvement: Prospecting is an ongoing process that requires continuous improvement. Salespeople should regularly review their prospecting strategies and techniques to identify areas for improvement and optimize their efforts.

Overall, effective prospecting is crucial for generating new business opportunities and driving sales growth. By using a combination of methods and strategies, salespeople can identify and qualify potential leads, build relationships, and ultimately, convert leads into customers.

2: Qualifying:

Once leads are identified, the next step is to qualify them to determine if they are a good fit for the product or service being offered. This involves understanding the customer's needs, budget, and decision-making process.

Qualifying leads is a crucial step in the sales process that helps salespeople determine which leads are most likely to become customers. Here's a detailed explanation of the qualifying process:

a: Definition: Qualifying leads involves assessing potential customers to determine if they have a genuine need for the product or service being offered, the budget to make a purchase, and the authority to make a buying decision. It helps salespeople prioritize their efforts and focus on leads that are most likely to convert.

b: Understanding Customer Needs: The first step in qualifying leads is to understand the customer's needs and challenges. This may involve asking probing questions to uncover their pain points and determine how the product or service can address their specific needs.

c: Assessing Budget: Salespeople need to determine if the lead has the budget to make a purchase. This may involve discussing pricing and budget constraints early in the sales process to ensure that both parties are aligned.

d: Identifying Decision-Makers: In B2B sales, it's important to identify the decision-makers within the organization who have the authority to make a buying decision. This may involve asking questions about the decision-making process and who else is involved in the buying process.

e: Qualification Criteria: Each business may have different criteria for qualifying leads based on their target market and product or service offering. Common criteria include the lead's need for the product or service, their budget, timeline for making a purchase, and decision-making authority.

f: Scoring Leads: Some businesses use lead scoring systems to prioritize leads based on their level of qualification. Leads are assigned a score based on factors such as their interest level, engagement with the sales team, and fit with the ideal customer profile.

g: Continuous Evaluation: Qualifying leads is an ongoing process that requires continuous evaluation and adjustment. Salespeople should regularly review their leads and update their qualification criteria based on feedback and changing market conditions.

By effectively qualifying leads, salespeople can focus their efforts on leads that are most likely to convert, leading to higher conversion rates and increased sales success.

3: Presenting:

After qualifying the lead, the salesperson presents the product or service to the customer. This may involve demonstrations, presentations, or proposals.

The presentation stage of the sales process is where the salesperson showcases the product or service to the qualified lead. This stage is crucial as it aims to address the specific needs and concerns of the lead and convince them that the product or service being offered is the best solution for their needs. Here's a detailed explanation of the presentation stage:

a:Preparation: Before the presentation, the salesperson should thoroughly prepare by reviewing the lead's needs and concerns identified during the qualification stage. They should also tailor the presentation to address these specific points.

b: Choosing the Right Format: The presentation can take various formats depending on the nature of the product or service and the preferences of the lead. It may involve a live demonstration, a formal presentation, a product walkthrough, or a proposal.

c: Demonstration: If the product or service is tangible, a demonstration can be a powerful way to showcase its features and benefits. The salesperson should highlight how the product or service addresses the lead's specific needs and solves their problems.

d: Presentation: A formal presentation can be used to provide detailed information about the product or service, its features, benefits, pricing, and any other relevant information. The presentation should be engaging and focused on the lead's needs and concerns.

e: Proposal: In some cases, the presentation may involve presenting a formal proposal outlining the terms of the offer, including pricing, terms and conditions, and any additional services or products included in the offer.

f: Handling Objections: During the presentation, the salesperson should be prepared to address any objections or concerns the lead may have. They should listen actively to the lead's feedback and respond with empathy and confidence.

g: Closing the Sale: The ultimate goal of the presentation is to close the sale. The salesperson should be prepared to ask for the sale and guide the lead through the next steps in the buying process.

h: Follow-Up: After the presentation, it's important for the salesperson to follow up with the lead to answer any remaining questions and address any concerns that may have arisen during the presentation. This helps to keep the momentum going and move the lead towards making a purchase decision.

Overall, the presentation stage is an opportunity for the salesperson to demonstrate the value of the product or service and build trust and confidence with the lead. By tailoring the presentation to address the lead's specific needs and concerns, the salesperson can increase the likelihood of closing the sale.

4: Handling objections:

During the sales process, customers may raise objections or concerns. The salesperson must be able to address these objections effectively to move the sale forward.

Handling objections is a critical skill for salespeople, as it allows them to address concerns or hesitations that potential customers may have and move the sales process forward. Here's a detailed explanation of how salespeople can effectively handle objections:

a: Understanding Objections: Salespeople should first listen carefully to the customer's objections to fully understand their concerns. Objections can arise for various reasons, such as price, product features, timing, or perceived risks.

b: Acknowledge and Empathize: It's essential for salespeople to acknowledge the customer's concerns and empathize with their perspective. This demonstrates understanding and builds rapport with the customer.

c: Clarify and Probe: Salespeople should ask clarifying questions to get to the root of the objection and understand the specific issue the customer is facing. Probing questions can help uncover additional information and provide insight into how to address the objection effectively.

d: Provide Information and Solutions: Once the objection is understood, salespeople should provide relevant information or solutions to address the customer's concerns. This may involve highlighting the features and benefits of the product or service, addressing misconceptions, or offering alternatives.

e: Handle Objections Proactively: Anticipating common objections and addressing them proactively during the presentation can help alleviate concerns before they arise. Salespeople can incorporate objection handling techniques into their presentations to preemptively address potential objections.

f: Use Social Proof: Providing evidence such as testimonials, case studies, or success stories can help build credibility and address objections related to product effectiveness or reliability. Social proof demonstrates that others have successfully overcome similar objections and achieved positive outcomes.

g: Stay Calm and Confident: It's essential for salespeople to remain calm and confident when handling objections. Confidence instills trust and reassures the customer that their concerns are being addressed effectively.

h: Close the Loop: After addressing the objection, salespeople should confirm with the customer that their concerns have been resolved satisfactorily and ask for their commitment to move forward in the sales process.

i: Follow-Up: If the objection requires further consideration or research, salespeople should follow up with the customer in a timely manner to provide additional information or address any remaining concerns. This demonstrates responsiveness and commitment to customer satisfaction.

By effectively handling objections, salespeople can overcome barriers to the sale, build trust with customers, and ultimately increase their chances of closing deals successfully.

5: Closing:

The final step in the sales process is closing the sale. This involves getting the customer to make a commitment to purchase the product or service.

Closing the sale is the culmination of all the efforts put into the sales process. It's the point where the salesperson asks for the customer's commitment to purchase the product or service. Here's a detailed explanation of the closing stage:

a: Recognizing Buying Signals: Throughout the sales process, the salesperson should be attentive to the customer's buying signals, which indicate their readiness to make a purchase. These signals can be verbal or non-verbal cues that show the customer's interest and intent to buy.

b: Choosing the Right Closing Technique: There are various closing techniques that salespeople can use based on the situation and the customer's buying behavior. Some common closing techniques include:

1: The assumptive close: Assuming the customer is ready to buy and asking for the sale.

2: The trial close: Asking a question to gauge the customer's readiness to buy, such as "Would you prefer the red or blue model?"

3: The summary close: Summarizing the key points of the discussion and asking for the sale based on the agreement reached.

c: Handling Objections: If the customer raises any final objections or concerns, the salesperson should address them promptly and effectively. Addressing objections at this stage is crucial to overcoming any remaining barriers to the sale.

d: Asking for the Sale: Once all objections have been addressed and the customer is ready to buy, the salesperson should confidently ask for the sale. This can be done using a direct question, such as "Can I process your order now?" or "Are you ready to move forward with this purchase?"

e: Closing the Deal: After asking for the sale, the salesperson should guide the customer through the final steps of the purchase process, such as completing the order form, signing a contract, or making a payment.

f: Handling Rejection: If the customer declines the offer, the salesperson should handle the rejection gracefully and respectfully. They can inquire about the reasons for the customer's decision and use this feedback to improve their sales approach in the future.

g: Follow-Up: After closing the sale, the salesperson should follow up with the customer to ensure their satisfaction and address any post-purchase concerns. This helps to build long-term relationships with customers and encourages repeat business.

By mastering the closing stage of the sales process, salespeople can increase their chances of successfully converting leads into customers and achieving their sales targets.

B: Setting Clear Objectives and Goals

Setting clear objectives and goals is essential for developing a successful sales strategy. Objectives are the specific outcomes that a salesperson wants to achieve, while goals are the measurable targets that will help them reach those objectives.

1: Objectives:

These can include increasing sales revenue, acquiring new customers, or expanding market share. Objectives should be specific, measurable, achievable, relevant, and time-bound (SMART).

Objectives are crucial in guiding the direction and focus of a sales strategy. They provide a clear roadmap for sales teams to follow and help measure the success of their efforts. Here's a detailed explanation of setting objectives in sales:

a: Specific: Objectives should be clear and specific, outlining exactly what is to be achieved. For example, instead of setting a general objective to "increase sales," a specific objective would be to "increase sales revenue by 20% in the next quarter."

b: Measurable: Objectives should be quantifiable so that progress can be tracked and measured. This allows sales teams to determine if they are on track to meet their goals or if adjustments need to be made. Using the example above, the objective is measurable because it specifies a 20% increase in sales revenue.

c: Achievable: Objectives should be realistic and attainable. While it's important to set ambitious goals, objectives should also be within the realm of possibility based on available resources and market conditions. Setting unrealistic objectives can demotivate sales teams and lead to frustration.

d: Relevant: Objectives should be aligned with the overall goals and strategies of the business. They should directly contribute to the success of the organization and be relevant to current market conditions and customer needs.

e: Time-bound: Objectives should have a specific timeframe for achievement. This helps create a sense of urgency and provides a deadline for action. Using the example above, the objective is time-bound because it specifies achieving a 20% increase in sales revenue within the next quarter.

Setting SMART objectives helps sales teams stay focused and motivated, provides a clear benchmark for success, and enables effective tracking and measurement of progress. By aligning objectives with the overall goals of the business, sales teams can work towards achieving long-term success and growth.

2: Goals:

Goals are the specific targets that a salesperson sets to achieve their objectives. For example, a salesperson may set a goal to increase sales revenue by 20% in the next quarter.

Goals are the specific targets that salespeople set to achieve their objectives. While objectives provide a broader direction, goals are more specific and measurable, providing a clear target for salespeople to aim for. Here's a detailed explanation of setting goals in sales:

a: Specific: Like objectives, goals should be specific and clearly defined. They should answer the questions of who, what, when, where, and why. For example, a goal to "increase sales revenue" is not specific enough. A more specific goal would be to "increase sales revenue by 20% in the next quarter."

b: Measurable: Goals should be quantifiable so that progress can be tracked and measured. This allows salespeople to determine if they are on track to meet their goals or if adjustments need to be made. Using the example above, the goal is measurable because it specifies a 20% increase in sales revenue.

c: Achievable: Goals should be realistic and attainable. While it's important to set ambitious goals, they should also be within the realm of possibility based on available resources and market conditions. Setting unrealistic goals can demotivate salespeople and lead to frustration.

d: Relevant: Goals should be aligned with the overall objectives and strategies of the business. They should directly contribute to the success of the organization and be relevant to current market conditions and customer needs.

e: Time-bound: Goals should have a specific timeframe for achievement. This helps create a sense of urgency and provides a deadline for action. Using the example above, the goal is time-bound because it specifies achieving a 20% increase in sales revenue within the next quarter.

Setting SMART goals helps salespeople stay focused and motivated, provides a clear benchmark for success, and enables effective tracking and measurement of progress. By aligning goals with the overall objectives of the business, salespeople can work towards achieving long-term success and growth.

3: Strategies:

Once objectives and goals are set, the salesperson must develop strategies to achieve them. This may involve identifying target markets, developing pricing strategies, or implementing promotional campaigns.

Strategies are the detailed plans and approaches that salespeople develop to achieve their objectives and goals. They outline the specific actions that will be taken to reach the desired outcomes. Here's a detailed explanation of developing strategies in sales:

a: Identifying Target Markets: One of the key strategies in sales is to identify and target specific market segments that are most likely to be interested in the product or service. This involves conducting market research to understand customer needs, preferences, and behaviors.

b: Developing Pricing Strategies: Pricing strategies play a crucial role in sales success. Salespeople need to determine the optimal pricing strategy based on factors such as product costs, competitor pricing, and customer perceptions of value. This may involve setting prices to maximize profitability, gain market share, or penetrate new markets.

c: Implementing Promotional Campaigns: Promotional campaigns are used to create awareness, generate interest, and drive sales of a product or service. Salespeople need to develop effective promotional strategies that reach the target market and communicate the value proposition of the product or service.

d: Creating Sales Presentations and Materials: Salespeople need to develop compelling sales presentations and materials that effectively communicate the benefits of the product or service to potential customers. This may include brochures, presentations, demos, and other sales collateral.

e: Building Relationships: Building strong relationships with customers is a key strategy in sales. This involves providing excellent customer service, understanding customer needs, and maintaining regular communication to build trust and loyalty.

f: Utilizing Technology: Technology plays an increasingly important role in sales strategies. Salespeople can use technology tools such as customer relationship management (CRM) systems, sales automation software, and data analytics to streamline sales processes, improve efficiency, and gain insights into customer behavior.

g: Adapting to Market Trends: Sales strategies should be flexible and adaptable to changing market trends and customer preferences. Salespeople need to monitor market trends closely and adjust their strategies accordingly to stay competitive.

By developing and implementing effective strategies, salespeople can increase their chances of achieving their objectives and goals, driving sales growth, and contributing to the overall success of the business.

C: Defining Target Markets and Ideal Customers

Defining target markets and ideal customers is critical for tailoring sales strategies to specific customer segments.

1: Target Markets: These are specific groups of customers that a business aims to reach with its products or services. Target markets can be defined based on demographics, psychographics, or behavior.

Target markets are specific groups of customers that a business aims to reach with its products or services. Identifying target markets is essential for developing effective marketing and sales strategies. Here's a detailed explanation of target markets:

a: Demographics: Demographic factors such as age, gender, income, education, occupation, and family status are commonly used to define target markets. For example, a company selling luxury watches may target affluent individuals aged 35-55.

b: Psychographics: Psychographic factors refer to customers' lifestyles, values, interests, and personality traits. This approach focuses on understanding customers' motivations and preferences. For example, a company selling outdoor gear may target adventurous individuals who enjoy outdoor activities.

c: Behavior: Behavioral factors include customers' purchasing behavior, brand loyalty, usage patterns, and response to marketing messages. This approach helps businesses understand how customers interact with their products or services. For example, a company may target customers who have previously purchased similar products or have shown interest in related products.

d: Geographic: Geographic factors refer to customers' location, such as country, region, city, or neighborhood. This approach is particularly relevant for businesses that offer products or services with local or regional appeal. For example, a restaurant may target customers in a specific neighborhood or city.

e: Target Market Segmentation: Businesses often use a combination of these factors to segment their target markets into smaller, more defined groups. This allows them to tailor their marketing and sales strategies to meet the specific needs and preferences of each segment. For example, a clothing retailer may target different segments based on age, gender, and style preferences.

f: Benefits of Identifying Target Markets: Identifying target markets helps businesses focus their resources and efforts on the most profitable customer segments. It allows them to tailor their products, pricing, distribution, and promotion strategies to meet the specific needs of their target customers. This targeted approach can lead to higher customer satisfaction, increased sales, and improved profitability.

Overall, identifying target markets is a critical step in developing successful marketing and sales strategies. By understanding the characteristics and preferences of their target customers, businesses can effectively reach and engage with their target markets, driving growth and success.

2: Ideal Customers: Ideal customers are those who are most likely to buy from a business. They may have specific needs, preferences, or characteristics that make them a good fit for the product or service being offered.

Ideal customers are the subset of the target market that are most likely to buy from a business. They are the customers who align perfectly with the business's offerings, values, and customer service standards. Here's a detailed explanation of ideal customers:

Specific Needs and Preferences: Ideal customers have specific needs, preferences, or challenges that align with the solutions offered by the business. For example, a software company may identify small businesses with limited IT resources as ideal customers for their affordable and easy-to-use software solutions.

a: Good Fit for the Product or Service: Ideal customers are a good fit for the product or service being offered. They see value in the offering and are willing to pay for it. For example, a luxury car manufacturer may identify affluent individuals who value quality and prestige as ideal customers for their high-end vehicles.

b: Likelihood to Purchase: Ideal customers are more likely to purchase from the business compared to other segments of the target market. They may have a higher level of interest or urgency in solving their problem or meeting their needs. For example, a travel agency may identify individuals planning a honeymoon as ideal customers for their honeymoon travel packages.

c: Characteristics and Traits: Ideal customers may share certain characteristics or traits that make them a good fit for the business. This could include demographics such as age, gender, income level, or psychographics such as lifestyle, values, and interests. For example, a fitness apparel brand may identify health-conscious individuals who enjoy active lifestyles as ideal customers for their products.

d: Lifetime Value: Ideal customers have the potential to generate significant value for the business over the long term. They are likely to make repeat purchases, refer others to the business, and become loyal customers. For example, a subscription-based service may identify customers who value convenience and are willing to pay a monthly fee for ongoing access to the service as ideal customers.

Identifying ideal customers helps businesses focus their marketing and sales efforts on the most promising opportunities. By understanding the needs, preferences, and characteristics of their ideal customers, businesses can tailor their messaging, offerings, and customer experience to attract and retain these valuable customers.

3: Segmentation: Once target markets and ideal customers are defined, the salesperson can segment them into smaller, more manageable groups. This allows for more targeted marketing and sales efforts.

Segmentation is the process of dividing a broad target market into smaller, more defined groups based on specific characteristics. This allows businesses to tailor their marketing and sales efforts to better meet the needs of each segment. Here's a detailed explanation of segmentation in sales:

a: Types of Segmentation:

1: Demographic Segmentation: Dividing the market based on demographic factors such as age, gender, income, education, and family status.

2: Psychographic Segmentation: Dividing the market based on lifestyle, values, interests, and personality traits.

3: Behavioral Segmentation: Dividing the market based on purchasing behavior, brand loyalty, product usage, and response to marketing messages.

4: Geographic Segmentation: Dividing the market based on geographic factors such as location, climate, culture, and population density.

b: Benefits of Segmentation:

1: Targeted Marketing: Segmentation allows businesses to tailor their marketing messages and campaigns to specific segments, increasing the likelihood of reaching the right audience with the right message.

2: Improved Customer Understanding: Segmentation helps businesses gain a deeper understanding of their customers' needs, preferences, and behaviors, allowing them to develop products and services that better meet customer needs.

3: Higher Conversion Rates: By targeting specific segments with tailored marketing efforts, businesses can increase the likelihood of converting leads into customers.

4: Increased Customer Loyalty: Segmenting customers based on their needs and preferences can help businesses build stronger relationships with their customers, leading to increased loyalty and repeat business.

c: Segmentation Strategies:

1: Mass Marketing: Targeting the entire market with a standardized marketing message. This approach is most effective for products or services with broad appeal.

2: Differentiated Marketing: Targeting multiple segments with different marketing messages and strategies. This approach is effective for businesses with diverse product lines or target markets.

3: Niche Marketing: Targeting a small, specialized segment of the market with unique products or services. This approach is effective for businesses serving niche markets with specific needs.

d: Implementation:

1: Businesses can implement segmentation by collecting and analyzing data about their target market and customer base. This may involve conducting market research, analyzing customer feedback, and using data analytics tools to identify relevant segments.

2: Once segments are identified, businesses can develop tailored marketing strategies and campaigns for each segment, focusing on addressing their specific needs and preferences.

Segmentation is a powerful tool for businesses to better understand their customers and tailor their marketing and sales efforts to maximize effectiveness. By segmenting their target market into smaller, more manageable groups, businesses can increase customer engagement, improve customer satisfaction, and drive sales growth.

In conclusion, understanding the sales process, setting clear objectives and goals, and defining target markets and ideal customers are foundational elements of a successful sales strategy. By focusing on these areas, salespeople can develop strategies that are more effective in achieving their sales goals.

Chapter 2: Market Analysis and Competitive Intelligence

A: Conducting Market Research

1: Market research is indeed a fundamental aspect of any successful sales strategy. It serves as the foundation for understanding the market landscape, customer behaviors, and competitive dynamics. This comprehensive process involves gathering and analyzing a wide range of information related to the market, including its size, growth trends, customer segments, and buying behavior. By delving into these key aspects, businesses can gain invaluable insights that inform their sales and marketing strategies, ultimately leading to more targeted and effective approaches.

2: Various methods are employed in market research to gather pertinent information. These methods include:

a: Surveys: Surveys are structured questionnaires designed to collect data from a sample of respondents. They can be conducted through online platforms, phone interviews, or in-person interactions. Surveys allow businesses to gather quantitative data on customer preferences, satisfaction levels, and purchasing habits.

b: Interviews: Interviews involve direct one-on-one conversations with individuals to gain deeper insights into their thoughts, opinions, and experiences. Unlike surveys, interviews offer the flexibility to probe further and explore nuanced responses. This qualitative approach provides valuable context and understanding of customer motivations and behaviors.

c: Focus Groups: Focus groups bring together a small, representative group of individuals to participate in a guided discussion facilitated by a moderator. This method allows businesses to explore topics in-depth, uncovering insights into customer attitudes, perceptions, and preferences. Focus groups are particularly useful for testing new product concepts, refining messaging, and gaining feedback on marketing campaigns.

d: Data Analysis: Data analysis involves examining existing data sources, such as sales data, customer databases, and market reports, to extract meaningful insights. Statistical techniques and analytical tools are used to identify patterns, trends, and correlations within the data. This quantitative approach provides valuable insights into market trends, customer behaviors, and competitive dynamics.

3: The ultimate goal of conducting market research is to gain actionable insights that drive informed decision-making. By analyzing the gathered information, sales teams can:

a: Identify New Opportunities: Market research helps businesses uncover untapped market segments, emerging trends, and unmet customer needs. By identifying new opportunities, sales teams can tailor their offerings and strategies to capitalize on these potential growth areas.

b: Understand Customer Pain Points: By delving into customer preferences, challenges, and pain points, market research enables businesses to better understand the needs and desires of their target audience. This understanding allows sales teams to develop solutions that address customer pain points more effectively, ultimately leading to higher levels of customer satisfaction and loyalty.

c: Tailor Messaging and Offerings: Armed with insights from market research, sales teams can tailor their messaging, product features, and pricing strategies to better resonate with their target audience. By aligning offerings with customer needs and preferences, businesses can enhance their competitive advantage and increase their chances of success in the market.

In summary, conducting market research is a critical step in developing a successful sales strategy. By leveraging various research methods to gather and analyze information, businesses can gain valuable insights that inform their decision-making and drive success in the marketplace.

B: Analyzing Competitors

1: Competitor analysis is a crucial component of a comprehensive sales strategy as it provides insights into the competitive landscape. This analysis involves evaluating competitors' strengths, weaknesses, opportunities, and threats (SWOT) to identify areas where a business can differentiate itself and gain a competitive edge. By understanding the competitive landscape, sales teams can develop strategies that capitalize on opportunities and mitigate potential threats.

2: There are several key aspects of competitors that sales teams should analyze:

a: Products and Services: Understanding competitors' offerings helps businesses identify gaps in the market and areas where they can differentiate themselves. This analysis includes examining product features, quality, pricing, and positioning.

b: Pricing Strategies: Analyzing competitors' pricing strategies provides insights into pricing trends in the market. It helps businesses determine whether they should match, undercut, or premium-price their products or services.

c: Marketing Campaigns: Reviewing competitors' marketing campaigns helps businesses understand how competitors are positioning themselves in the market and targeting customers. This analysis can inform businesses' own marketing strategies and messaging.

d: Customer Feedback: Monitoring customer feedback and reviews of competitors' products or services can provide valuable insights into customer preferences and pain points. This information can help businesses tailor their offerings to better meet customer needs.

3: Competitor analysis enables sales teams to anticipate competitors' moves and develop strategies to counter them. For example:

a: Offering Better Pricing: If competitors are offering lower prices, businesses can explore ways to offer better value or differentiate their offerings to justify higher prices.

b: Improving Product Features: Identifying areas where competitors' products fall short allows businesses to enhance their own products' features to meet customer needs more effectively.

c: Enhancing Customer Service: If competitors are known for their exceptional customer service, businesses can focus on improving their own customer service to compete more effectively.

By conducting thorough competitor analysis, sales teams can gain a deeper understanding of the competitive landscape and position their products or services more effectively in the market. This analysis helps businesses identify opportunities for growth, develop strategies to differentiate themselves from competitors, and ultimately achieve greater success in the marketplace.

C: Identifying Opportunities and Threats

1: Market analysis plays a crucial role in helping sales teams identify opportunities for growth and expansion. By analyzing market trends, customer needs, and competitive dynamics, sales teams can uncover potential opportunities that align with the business's strengths and capabilities. Some key aspects of identifying opportunities include:

a: **Underserved Market Segments**: Market analysis helps businesses identify market segments that are currently underserved or overlooked by competitors. By targeting these segments, businesses can gain a competitive edge and increase market share.

b: **Emerging Trends**: Market analysis helps businesses stay ahead of emerging trends in the market. By identifying and capitalizing on these trends early, businesses can position themselves as industry leaders and attract new customers.

c: **Gaps in the Market**: Market analysis helps businesses identify gaps or unmet needs in the market. By developing products or services that address these gaps, businesses can create new revenue streams and expand their customer base.

2: Market analysis also helps sales teams identify potential threats to the business. By understanding the competitive landscape, market dynamics, and external factors that could impact the business, sales teams can develop strategies to mitigate these risks. Some key aspects of identifying threats include:

a: New Competitors: Market analysis helps businesses monitor the competitive landscape for new entrants. By identifying new competitors early, businesses can develop strategies to protect their market share and retain customers.

b: Changes in Consumer Preferences: Market analysis helps businesses stay informed about changes in consumer preferences and buying behavior. By adapting their offerings to meet these changing preferences, businesses can remain competitive and retain customer loyalty.

c: Economic Downturns: Market analysis helps businesses anticipate economic downturns or other external factors that could impact consumer spending. By developing contingency plans and diversifying their revenue streams, businesses can mitigate the impact of these threats.

By conducting thorough market analysis, sales teams can identify opportunities for growth and expansion, as well as potential threats to the business. This information allows businesses to develop strategies that capitalize on opportunities and mitigate risks, ultimately driving long-term success and profitability.

Overall, conducting market analysis and competitive intelligence is essential for sales teams to understand the market landscape, identify opportunities for growth, and stay ahead of competitors. By gathering and analyzing relevant data, sales teams can make informed decisions that drive sales and contribute to the overall success of the business.

Chapter 3: Building a Strong Sales Team

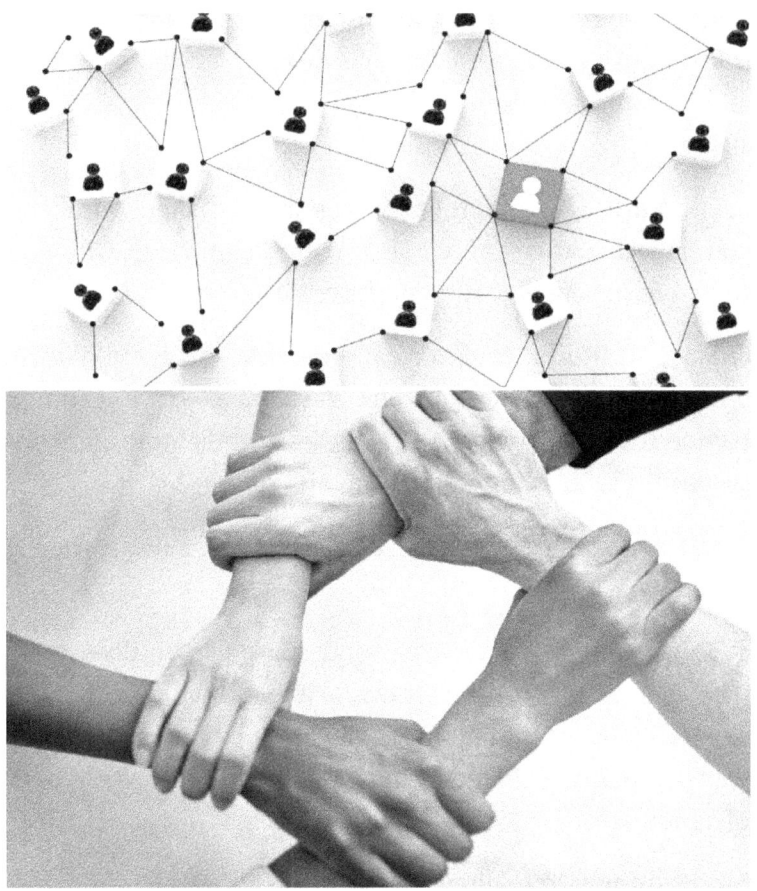

A: Recruiting and Hiring the Right Talent

1: Building a strong sales team starts with recruiting and hiring the right talent. This involves identifying candidates who not only possess the necessary skills and experience but also align with the company's culture, values, and sales objectives. Hiring the right talent can significantly impact a team's performance and overall success. Key considerations in recruiting and hiring include:

a: Skills and Experience: Look for candidates with relevant sales experience and a track record of success in similar roles. Consider the specific skills needed for the role, such as communication, negotiation, and relationship-building skills.

b: Cultural Fit: Ensure that candidates align with the company's culture and values. A good cultural fit can lead to higher job satisfaction and retention rates.

c: Sales Aptitude: Look for candidates who have a natural aptitude for sales, such as resilience, drive, and a competitive spirit. These traits are often indicators of future success in sales roles.

2: The recruitment process typically involves several stages, including:

a: Job Postings: Create clear and compelling job postings that outline the role's responsibilities, qualifications, and expectations. Post the job on relevant job boards, company website, and social media channels to attract a diverse pool of candidates.

b: Resume Screening: Review resumes to shortlist candidates who meet the basic qualifications for the role. Look for relevant sales experience, skills, and achievements.

c: Interviews: Conduct interviews to assess candidates' fit for the role and company culture. Ask behavioral questions to gauge their past performance and problem-solving skills. Consider using panel interviews to get multiple perspectives on each candidate.

d: Reference Checks: Contact references provided by the candidates to verify their qualifications and work experience. This step helps ensure that the candidate's background aligns with what they have presented during the interview process.

3: Companies can also use assessments or tests to evaluate candidates' sales aptitude and potential. These assessments can help identify candidates who have the right qualities and traits for sales roles, such as communication skills, resilience, and problem-solving abilities. Assessments can be especially useful for identifying candidates with high potential who may not have a traditional sales background.

By investing time and effort into recruiting and hiring the right talent, companies can build a strong sales team that drives revenue growth and achieves long-term success.

B: Training and Developing Sales Skills

1: Providing ongoing training and development is essential for ensuring that sales team members have the skills and knowledge needed to excel in their roles. Effective training programs can help improve sales performance, boost morale, and increase employee retention. Key considerations for training and development include:

a: Continuous Learning: Encourage a culture of continuous learning and development within the sales team. Sales professionals should be encouraged to seek out new learning opportunities and stay updated on industry trends and best practices.

b: Individual Development Plans: Work with each sales team member to create an individual development plan that aligns with their career goals and development needs. This can include specific training courses, workshops, or certifications that will help them grow in their role.

c: Feedback and Coaching: Provide regular feedback and coaching to sales team members to help them improve their skills and performance. Coaching sessions can focus on areas for improvement identified through performance evaluations or sales metrics.

2: Sales training programs should cover a range of topics to help sales team members develop the skills and knowledge needed to succeed in their roles. Some key areas to focus on include:

a: Product Knowledge: Ensure that sales team members have a deep understanding of the products or services they are selling. This includes understanding the features and benefits of the products, as well as how they meet customer needs.

b: Sales Techniques: Provide training on effective sales techniques, such as prospecting, qualifying leads, delivering pitches, handling objections, and closing deals. Sales team members should be equipped with a variety of strategies to engage with customers and drive sales.

c: Customer Relationship Management: Train sales team members on how to build and maintain strong relationships with customers. This includes effective communication, understanding customer needs, and providing excellent customer service.

d: Negotiation Skills: Provide training on negotiation techniques to help sales team members secure deals and win business. This includes understanding customer needs, finding win-win solutions, and handling objections effectively.

3: Training can be delivered through a variety of methods, including:

a: Workshops and Seminars: Conduct in-person or virtual workshops and seminars to provide hands-on training and interactive learning experiences.

b: Online Courses: Offer online courses or webinars that sales team members can complete at their own pace to improve their skills and knowledge.

c: Mentoring: Pair less experienced sales team members with more experienced mentors who can provide guidance, support, and coaching.

d: On-the-Job Training: Provide opportunities for on-the-job training, where sales team members can learn new skills and techniques while working on real-world sales projects.

By investing in training and development, businesses can empower their sales team members to perform at their best, drive revenue growth, and achieve long-term success.

C: Motivating and Managing Salespeople

1: Motivating and managing salespeople effectively requires a deep understanding of their individual needs, goals, and motivators. Each salesperson is unique, and what motivates one may not necessarily motivate another.

Therefore, it's essential for sales managers to take the time to get to know their team members and tailor their approach to each individual.

a: Understanding Individual Needs: Sales managers should take the time to understand each salesperson's personal and professional goals, as well as their strengths, weaknesses, and areas for development. This understanding can help managers tailor their management approach to each individual, providing the support and guidance they need to succeed.

b: Setting Realistic Goals: Set clear, achievable goals for salespeople that align with both their individual goals and the overall goals of the organization. Goals should be challenging yet attainable, providing motivation for salespeople to strive for excellence.

2: Salespeople are often motivated by incentives such as bonuses, commissions, and recognition. These incentives can be powerful motivators and can help drive sales performance. Some key considerations for motivating salespeople include:

a: Financial Incentives: Offer competitive commission structures, bonuses, and other financial incentives to reward sales performance. These incentives should be tied to clear, measurable goals to ensure they are motivating and aligned with the company's objectives.

b: Recognition and Rewards: Recognize and reward top performers publicly to reinforce positive behaviors and motivate others. This can include shout-outs in team meetings, awards ceremonies, or other forms of recognition that highlight individual and team achievements.

3: Effective sales management involves setting clear expectations, providing regular feedback and coaching, and creating a positive and supportive work environment. Some key strategies for managing salespeople include:

a: **Setting Clear Expectations**: Clearly communicate performance expectations, goals, and objectives to salespeople. Ensure they understand what is expected of them and how their performance will be measured.

b: **Providing Regular Feedback**: Provide constructive feedback on a regular basis to help salespeople improve their performance. This feedback should be specific, actionable, and focused on behaviors that can be changed.

c: **Coaching and Development**: Offer coaching and development opportunities to help salespeople improve their skills and reach their full potential. This can include one-on-one coaching sessions, training programs, and mentorship opportunities.

4: By motivating and managing salespeople effectively, companies can improve performance, increase sales, and reduce turnover. A motivated and engaged sales team is more likely to achieve its goals and contribute to the overall success of the organization.

Chapter 4: Developing a Sales Plan

A: Setting Sales Targets and Quotas

1: Setting sales targets and quotas is a fundamental aspect of sales management, providing sales teams with clear goals to work towards. These targets help align sales efforts with the overall objectives of the organization and provide a benchmark for measuring performance. Key considerations for setting sales targets and quotas include:

a: Alignment with Business Objectives: Sales targets should be aligned with the broader goals and objectives of the organization. This ensures that sales efforts are focused on activities that drive business growth and profitability.

b: Challenging Yet Achievable: Targets should be challenging enough to motivate sales teams to perform at their best, but also achievable with the right effort and resources. Unrealistically high targets can demotivate sales teams and lead to burnout.

2: Targets are typically set based on a variety of factors, including historical data, market trends, and company objectives. Sales managers may analyze past sales performance, market conditions, and competitor activities to set realistic targets. Some key considerations for setting sales targets include:

a: Historical Data: Analyzing past sales performance can provide insights into trends and patterns that can help inform future targets. This includes understanding seasonal fluctuations, product performance, and customer behavior.

b: Market Trends: Keeping abreast of market trends and industry developments can help sales managers set targets that reflect current market conditions. This may include changes in customer preferences, competitive activities, and economic factors.

c: Company Objectives: Sales targets should be aligned with the broader objectives of the organization, such as revenue targets, market share goals, or product launch targets. This ensures that sales efforts are contributing to the overall success of the business.

3: Quotas are specific targets assigned to individual salespeople or teams. Quotas help track performance at a granular level and ensure accountability. Some key considerations for setting quotas include:

a: Individual Performance: Quotas should be tailored to reflect each salesperson's individual capabilities and responsibilities. This ensures that quotas are fair and achievable for each team member.

b: Team Dynamics: For team-based quotas, it's important to consider the dynamics within the team and how individual contributions add up to the team's overall target. This encourages collaboration and teamwork.

4: Sales targets and quotas should be regularly reviewed and adjusted as needed to reflect changes in the market or business conditions. This ensures that targets remain relevant and achievable, even as external factors change. Regular reviews also provide an opportunity to identify and address any issues or challenges that may be impacting performance.

B: Creating a Sales Forecast

1: A sales forecast is a crucial tool for businesses to estimate future sales revenue based on past sales data, market trends, and other relevant factors. It provides valuable insights that help businesses plan and allocate resources effectively, anticipate demand, and set realistic goals. A well-prepared sales forecast can serve as a roadmap for the sales team and the entire organization.

2: Sales forecasts play a critical role in strategic planning and decision-making. They help businesses determine the level of production, inventory, and staffing needed to meet future demand. Additionally, sales forecasts can help businesses identify potential opportunities and challenges in the market, allowing them to adjust their strategies accordingly.

3: There are two main approaches to creating a sales forecast:

a: Quantitative Methods: These methods involve analyzing historical sales data and using statistical techniques such as trend analysis, regression analysis, and time series analysis to predict future sales. Quantitative methods are based on mathematical models and provide a quantitative estimate of future sales.

b: Qualitative Methods: These methods rely on expert opinion, market research, and other non-quantitative data to predict future sales. Qualitative methods are often used when there is limited historical data or when external factors (such as changes in the market or regulatory environment) are expected to have a significant impact on sales.

4: It's important to regularly review and update the sales forecast to ensure its accuracy and relevance. As market conditions and business environments change, forecasts may need to be adjusted to reflect these changes. By regularly updating the sales forecast, businesses can better anticipate and respond to changes in the market, ultimately improving their overall performance and competitiveness.

C: Allocating Resources and Budget

1: Allocating resources and budget is a critical aspect of sales strategy that involves determining how to best allocate sales resources, such as personnel, equipment, and marketing materials, to achieve sales targets. Effective resource allocation ensures that sales teams have the necessary tools and support to perform at their best and drive revenue growth.

2: Budgeting is an integral part of resource allocation and involves estimating the costs associated with achieving sales targets and ensuring that sufficient funds are available to support sales activities. A well-prepared sales budget should take into account all relevant costs, including personnel costs, marketing expenses, travel and entertainment expenses, and any other costs associated with sales operations.

3: When allocating resources and budgeting for sales, it's important to consider the following factors:

a: Alignment with Business Objectives: Sales budgets should be aligned with overall business objectives and strategies. This ensures that sales efforts are focused on activities that will help achieve the company's goals.

b: Market Conditions: Market conditions can have a significant impact on sales performance. It's important to consider factors such as market growth, competition, and customer demand when allocating resources and budgeting for sales.

c: Expected Return on Investment (ROI): It's essential to evaluate the expected ROI of sales activities when allocating resources and budgeting. This helps ensure that resources are allocated to activities that will deliver the greatest return.

4: By effectively allocating resources and budget, businesses can optimize their sales efforts and maximize revenue. This involves continuously monitoring and evaluating the effectiveness of sales activities and making adjustments as needed to ensure that resources are being used efficiently and effectively.

Chapter 5: Crafting a Compelling Value Proposition

A: Understanding Customer Needs

1: Understanding customer needs is crucial for developing a compelling value proposition that resonates with target customers. It involves identifying what customers want, what problems they need to solve, and what benefits they seek from a product or service. By understanding these needs, businesses can tailor their offerings to better meet customer expectations and differentiate themselves from competitors.

2: There are several methods that businesses can use to understand customer needs:

a: Market Research: Conducting market research allows businesses to gather data on customer preferences, behaviors, and buying patterns. This information can help businesses identify trends and anticipate future customer needs.

b: Customer Surveys: Surveys can be used to gather direct feedback from customers about their needs, preferences, and satisfaction levels. Surveys can provide valuable insights that can be used to improve products or services and enhance the customer experience.

c: Analysis of Customer Feedback: Analyzing customer feedback, such as reviews, complaints, and suggestions, can provide valuable insights into customer needs and pain points. This information can be used to make improvements to products or services and address customer concerns.

d: Analysis of Buying Behavior: Analyzing customer buying behavior can help businesses understand what motivates customers to make a purchase. This information can be used to tailor marketing messages and sales strategies to better meet customer needs.

3: By understanding customer needs, businesses can develop products or services that are more likely to resonate with customers and meet their expectations. This can lead to increased customer satisfaction, loyalty, and ultimately, business success. Understanding customer needs also allows businesses to differentiate themselves from competitors by offering unique value propositions that address specific customer needs and preferences.

B: Communicating Unique Selling Points

1: Communicating unique selling points (USPs) is essential for crafting a compelling value proposition that differentiates a product or service from competitors. USPs are the characteristics or features of a product or service that set it apart and make it stand out in the eyes of the customer. By highlighting these unique features, businesses can attract customers and convince them of the value of their offerings.

2: To effectively communicate USPs, businesses should:

a: Clearly Articulate USPs: Clearly communicate the unique features and benefits of the product or service in marketing materials, sales pitches, and other communications. This helps customers understand what sets the product or service apart and why it is a better choice than competitors.

b: Use Compelling Messaging: Use compelling messaging that resonates with the target market and emphasizes the benefits of the product or service. This can include highlighting key features, advantages over competitors, and how the product or service solves customer problems or meets their needs.

c: Highlight Value Proposition: Clearly articulate the value proposition of the product or service, focusing on how it addresses customer pain points, improves their lives, or fulfills specific needs.

3: USPs should be relevant to the target market and emphasize the benefits of the product or service to the customer. When communicating USPs, businesses should consider the following:

a: Target Audience: Tailor messaging to resonate with the target audience's needs, preferences, and values. Understand what motivates them and how the product or service can address their specific needs or challenges.

b: Competitive Landscape: Position USPs in a way that highlights how the product or service is superior to competitors. This can include emphasizing unique features, better performance, or greater value for money.

c: Customer Benefits: Focus on the benefits that the product or service provides to the customer. This can include saving time or money, improving quality of life, or enhancing convenience.

By effectively communicating USPs, businesses can create a strong value proposition that resonates with customers and sets their offerings apart from competitors. This can lead to increased customer interest, loyalty, and ultimately, sales.

C: Creating Persuasive Sales Messages

1: Creating persuasive sales messages is essential for capturing the attention of the target audience and convincing them of the value of a product or service. Persuasive sales messages use language and imagery that resonate with the target audience, addressing their needs, wants, and pain points. These messages should be compelling and convincing, prompting the audience to take action.

2: To create persuasive sales messages, businesses should:

a: Highlight Benefits: Focus on the benefits of the product or service rather than just its features. Explain how the product or service can solve customer problems or improve their lives.

b: Address Pain Points: Identify and address customer pain points in the sales message. Show how the product or service can alleviate these pain points and provide solutions.

c: Use Persuasive Language: Use persuasive language that evokes emotion and prompts action. Use words that convey value, urgency, and exclusivity to compel the audience to take action.

3: Tailoring sales messages to different customer segments and communication channels is important for maximum impact. Different customers may have different needs, preferences, and communication styles, so messages should be adapted to resonate with each segment. Messages should also be tailored to suit the specific communication channel, whether it's email, social media, or in-person communication.

4: By crafting persuasive sales messages, businesses can effectively communicate their value proposition and persuade customers to buy. Persuasive sales messages can help businesses stand out in a crowded marketplace, capture the attention of potential customers, and drive sales and revenue.

Chapter 6: Sales Process Optimization

A: Mapping the Sales Process

1: Mapping the sales process is a critical step in developing an efficient and effective sales strategy. It involves defining and documenting each step involved in the sales journey, from lead generation to closing the sale. By mapping out the sales process, sales teams can gain a better understanding of the overall flow of the process and identify areas where improvements can be made to streamline operations and improve sales performance.

2: Key benefits of mapping the sales process include:

a: Understanding the Sales Journey: Mapping the sales process helps sales teams understand the journey that customers take from initial contact to final purchase. This understanding allows sales teams to align their efforts with customer needs and expectations, leading to more successful sales outcomes.

b: Identifying Key Milestones: By mapping the sales process, sales teams can identify key milestones or touchpoints in the sales journey. These milestones help track progress and provide opportunities for sales teams to engage with customers and move them closer to making a purchase.

c: Improving Efficiency: Mapping the sales process helps identify areas where the sales process can be streamlined or automated to improve efficiency. By eliminating unnecessary steps or bottlenecks, sales teams can improve their productivity and focus on activities that drive sales.

3: When mapping the sales process, it's important to create a map that is clear, easy to follow, and includes the following elements for each step:

a: Inputs: Identify the inputs or resources required for each step in the sales process. This could include lead lists, marketing materials, or customer information.

b: Outputs: Determine the outputs or outcomes of each step in the sales process. This could include qualified leads, sales proposals, or closed deals.

c: Responsibilities: Clearly define the responsibilities of each team member involved in the sales process. This helps ensure accountability and transparency throughout the sales journey.

By mapping the sales process and clearly defining each step, inputs, outputs, and responsibilities, sales teams can improve their overall efficiency, effectiveness, and success in closing deals and driving revenue.

B: Identifying Bottlenecks and Opportunities for Improvement

1: Identifying bottlenecks and areas for improvement in the sales process is crucial for optimizing sales performance. Bottlenecks are points in the sales process where the flow of work is hindered or slowed down, leading to inefficiencies and delays. By identifying and addressing these bottlenecks, businesses can improve sales productivity, shorten sales cycles, and ultimately increase revenue.

2: Common bottlenecks in the sales process include:

a: Long Sales Cycles: Sales cycles that are too long can lead to lost opportunities and increased costs. Identifying the reasons for long sales cycles, such as ineffective lead nurturing or complex decision-making processes, can help businesses streamline their processes and accelerate sales.

b: Inefficient Lead Qualification Processes: If leads are not effectively qualified, sales teams may waste time and resources pursuing leads that are unlikely to convert. Improving lead qualification processes can help focus sales efforts on high-potential leads and improve conversion rates.

c: Poor Communication Between Sales and Marketing Teams: Lack of alignment between sales and marketing teams can lead to missed opportunities and ineffective marketing campaigns. Improving communication and collaboration between these teams can help ensure that marketing efforts are targeted towards the right audience and support the sales process effectively.

3: Opportunities for improvement in the sales process may include:

a: Streamlining Workflows: Simplifying and streamlining sales processes can help reduce complexity and improve efficiency. This may involve automating repetitive tasks, eliminating unnecessary steps, or standardizing processes across the sales team.

b: Implementing New Technologies: Adopting new technologies, such as customer relationship management (CRM) systems, sales automation tools, or data analytics software, can help improve sales efficiency and effectiveness. These tools can provide valuable insights into customer behavior, streamline communication, and help sales teams prioritize leads.

c: Providing Additional Training: Continuous training and development can help sales teams stay up-to-date with industry trends, improve their sales skills, and adapt to changing market conditions. Providing additional training opportunities can help sales teams perform at their best and achieve better results.

4: By addressing bottlenecks and improving efficiency in the sales process, businesses can increase sales productivity, shorten sales cycles, and ultimately drive revenue growth. Regularly reviewing and optimizing the sales process is essential for maintaining a competitive edge and achieving long-term success in sales.

C: Implementing Sales Automation and Technology

1: Sales automation and technology can significantly impact the sales process by streamlining workflows, improving efficiency, and enhancing the overall customer experience. These tools can automate repetitive tasks, track customer interactions, and provide valuable insights into sales performance, enabling sales teams to focus on high-value activities that drive revenue.

2: Examples of sales automation tools include:

a: Customer Relationship Management (CRM) Systems: CRM systems help businesses manage customer interactions, track leads, and organize sales activities. They provide a central database for storing customer information, making it easier for sales teams to access and use data to personalize interactions and improve customer relationships.

b: Email Marketing Platforms: Email marketing platforms automate the process of sending marketing emails to customers and prospects. These platforms can segment email lists, personalize messages, and track email performance, helping businesses engage with customers more effectively and drive sales.

c: Sales Analytics Software: Sales analytics software provides insights into sales performance, customer behavior, and market trends. By analyzing this data, businesses can identify opportunities for growth, optimize sales strategies, and make data-driven decisions to improve sales effectiveness.

3: Benefits of implementing sales automation and technology include:

a: Increased Efficiency: Sales automation tools can streamline workflows and eliminate manual tasks, saving time and resources for sales teams. This allows sales teams to focus on high-value activities, such as building relationships and closing deals.

b: Improved Customer Experience: By using data and analytics, businesses can personalize their interactions with customers, anticipate their needs, and provide a seamless buying experience. This can lead to increased customer satisfaction and loyalty.

c: Better Sales Performance: Sales automation tools can help businesses track sales performance metrics, such as conversion rates and sales cycle length, and identify areas for improvement. By optimizing sales processes and strategies, businesses can increase sales effectiveness and drive revenue growth.

4: By implementing sales automation and technology, businesses can reduce manual effort, increase sales effectiveness, and ultimately drive revenue growth. It's important for businesses to carefully evaluate their needs and choose the right tools and technologies that align with their sales objectives and customer expectations.

Chapter 7: Effective Sales Techniques

A: Building Rapport and Trust with Customers

1: Building rapport and trust with customers is essential for establishing a strong relationship and increasing the likelihood of a successful sale. Rapport is the sense of connection and understanding between two people, while trust is the belief that someone is reliable and honest. Both are crucial in sales, as they help create a positive customer experience and increase the chances of closing a deal.

2: Salespeople can build rapport with customers by:

a: Showing genuine interest: Salespeople should take the time to get to know their customers, asking about their needs, interests, and challenges. This shows that they care about the customer as an individual, not just as a potential sale.

b: Active listening: Listening carefully to customers' needs and concerns is key to building rapport. Salespeople should focus on understanding the customer's perspective and responding thoughtfully to their questions and comments.

c: Finding common ground: Building rapport is often about finding common interests or experiences that help establish a connection with the customer. Salespeople can use small talk to find common ground and create a more relaxed and friendly interaction.

3: Trust is built through:

a: Honesty: Salespeople should always be honest with customers, even if it means admitting a mistake or acknowledging a limitation. Customers appreciate honesty and are more likely to trust salespeople who are transparent and truthful.

b: Reliability: Salespeople should deliver on their promises and follow through on commitments. This helps demonstrate that they can be trusted to deliver a high-quality product or service.

4: Building rapport and trust takes time and effort, but it can lead to long-term customer loyalty and repeat business. Customers are more likely to buy from salespeople they trust and feel comfortable with, so investing in building strong relationships can pay off in the form of increased sales and a loyal customer base.

B: Overcoming Objections

1: Overcoming objections is a common challenge in sales, as customers may have concerns or doubts that prevent them from making a purchase. Objections can arise due to various reasons, such as price, product features, timing, or perceived risks. However, objections should be viewed as opportunities to address customer concerns and provide solutions that can lead to a successful sale.

2: Salespeople can overcome objections by:

a: Listening actively: When a customer raises an objection, it's essential to listen carefully to understand their concerns fully. This demonstrates empathy and shows the customer that their concerns are being taken seriously.

b: Addressing concerns directly: Salespeople should address objections directly and provide relevant information or evidence to support their response. This could include highlighting the benefits of the product or service, addressing misconceptions, or providing examples of satisfied customers.

c: Providing solutions: Salespeople should offer solutions to alleviate customer concerns. This could involve offering a discount or special promotion, providing a product demonstration or trial, or offering a guarantee or warranty to reduce perceived risks.

3: It's important for salespeople to remain calm, empathetic, and confident when handling objections. They should view objections as opportunities to further educate the customer about the product or service and strengthen the relationship. By addressing objections effectively, salespeople can build trust with customers and increase the likelihood of a successful sale.

C: Closing Deals and Securing Commitments

1: Closing deals is the final step in the sales process, where the salesperson asks the customer to make a purchase or commit to a decision. This step is crucial as it determines whether all the effort put into the sales process will result in a successful sale. Effective closing techniques are essential for convincing the customer to take action and finalize the deal.

2: Effective closing techniques include:

a: Summarizing Benefits: Remind the customer of the key benefits of the product or service and how it meets their needs or solves their problems. This reinforces the value proposition and helps the customer make a decision.

b: Creating a Sense of Urgency: Create a sense of urgency by highlighting limited-time offers, special promotions, or the benefits of acting quickly. This encourages the customer to make a decision sooner rather than later.

c: Offering Incentives: Offer incentives such as discounts, free trials, or additional services to sweeten the deal and encourage the customer to commit.

3: Salespeople should be prepared to handle objections and address any final concerns the customer may have before closing the deal. This may involve providing additional information, addressing misconceptions, or offering reassurances to alleviate any doubts the customer may have.

4: Securing commitments involves getting the customer to agree to take action, whether it's making a purchase, signing a contract, or scheduling a follow-up meeting. This step is crucial for ensuring that the sales process moves forward and that the customer is committed to the decision.

5: By mastering these techniques, salespeople can increase their success in closing deals and securing long-term commitments from customers. Effective closing techniques can help salespeople achieve their sales targets, build strong relationships with customers, and drive revenue growth for their business.

Chapter 8: Sales Metrics and Performance Tracking

A: Key Performance Indicators (KPIs) for Sales

1: Key Performance Indicators (KPIs) are measurable values that demonstrate how effectively a company is achieving its key business objectives. In sales, KPIs help track and evaluate the performance of sales teams and individuals, providing valuable insights into their effectiveness and contribution to the overall success of the business.

2: Common sales KPIs include:

a: Sales Revenue: Total revenue generated from sales. This KPI provides an overall measure of the effectiveness of the sales team in generating revenue for the business.

b: Sales Growth: Percentage increase in sales revenue over a specified period. This KPI helps track the growth trajectory of the business and indicates its ability to expand its customer base and increase market share.

c: Customer Acquisition Cost (CAC): The cost associated with acquiring a new customer. This KPI helps measure the efficiency of the sales and marketing efforts in acquiring new customers and can help identify opportunities to reduce costs.

d: Customer Lifetime Value (CLTV): The total revenue a company expects to earn from a customer throughout their relationship. This KPI helps businesses understand the long-term value of their customer relationships and can inform decisions about customer retention and loyalty programs.

e: Conversion Rate: The percentage of leads that result in a sale. This KPI helps measure the effectiveness of the sales team in converting leads into customers and can highlight areas for improvement in the sales process.

f: Sales Pipeline Velocity: The rate at which leads move through the sales pipeline. This KPI helps measure the efficiency of the sales process and can help identify bottlenecks or areas where leads are getting stuck.

3: By tracking these KPIs, sales teams can identify areas for improvement, set realistic targets, and measure their progress towards achieving their goals. KPIs provide a way to measure the effectiveness of sales strategies and tactics, allowing businesses to make data-driven decisions and optimize their sales performance.

B: Monitoring and Analyzing Sales Data

1: Monitoring and analyzing sales data is essential for identifying trends, patterns, and opportunities for improvement. Sales data provides valuable insights into the performance of sales teams, the effectiveness of sales strategies, and the overall health of the business.

2: Sales data can include information on sales revenue, customer demographics, sales cycle length, conversion rates, and more. By collecting and analyzing this data, businesses can gain a better understanding of their customers, their buying behavior, and their preferences.

3: Analyzing sales data can help businesses:

a: Identify Profitable Customer Segments: By analyzing sales data, businesses can identify their most profitable customer segments and tailor their marketing and sales efforts to target these segments more effectively.

b: Optimize Sales Processes: Sales data can help businesses identify bottlenecks or inefficiencies in the sales process and make improvements to streamline operations and improve sales performance.

c: Make Informed Decisions: Sales data provides a factual basis for decision-making, allowing businesses to make informed decisions about resource allocation, product development, pricing strategies, and more.

4: Sales data can be collected through various channels, such as CRM systems, sales reports, customer feedback, and sales analytics tools. By collecting and analyzing sales data regularly, businesses can stay ahead of the competition, adapt to changing market conditions, and drive revenue growth.

C: Continuous Improvement and Adaptation

1: Continuous improvement is the ongoing effort to improve products, services, or processes. In sales, continuous improvement is crucial for staying competitive and meeting the evolving needs of customers. It involves identifying areas for improvement, implementing changes, and measuring the impact of those changes to drive ongoing growth and success.

2: In sales, continuous improvement involves:

a: Identifying Areas for Improvement: Sales teams should regularly review sales metrics, such as conversion rates, average deal size, and sales cycle length, to identify areas for improvement. They should also gather feedback from customers and internal stakeholders to understand where changes may be needed.

b: Implementing Changes: Once areas for improvement are identified, sales teams should develop and implement changes to address these areas. This may involve updating sales processes, providing additional training for salespeople, or revising sales strategies.

c: Measuring Impact: After implementing changes, it's important to measure the impact of those changes on sales performance. This can help determine whether the changes were effective and identify further areas for improvement.

3: Sales teams should be open to feedback and willing to adapt their strategies based on changing market conditions, customer needs, and competitive pressures. This may involve:

a: Adapting to Changing Market Conditions: Sales teams should monitor market trends and adjust their strategies accordingly. For example, if a new competitor enters the market, sales teams may need to revise their pricing or marketing strategies to remain competitive.

b: Meeting Customer Needs: Customer preferences and needs can change over time. Sales teams should regularly engage with customers to understand their evolving needs and adjust their offerings and sales approaches accordingly.

c: Responding to Competitive Pressures: Sales teams should be aware of their competitors' strategies and be prepared to respond to competitive pressures. This may involve offering promotions or discounts to match competitors' prices or developing new features or services to differentiate their offerings.

4: By continuously improving and adapting, sales teams can stay ahead of the competition and achieve long-term success. Continuous improvement is not a one-time event but rather an ongoing process that requires commitment, dedication, and a willingness to learn and evolve.

Chapter 9: Sales Strategy in the Digital Age

A: Leveraging Social Media and Online Platforms

1: Social media and online platforms offer powerful tools for reaching and engaging with customers. These platforms have become essential components of sales strategies, allowing businesses to connect with their audience in a more direct and personalized way.

2: Sales teams can leverage social media platforms such as Facebook, Twitter, LinkedIn, and Instagram to connect with potential customers, share content, and build relationships. These platforms offer various features, such as targeted advertising, messaging, and content sharing, that can help sales teams reach their target audience more effectively.

3: Social media listening tools can help sales teams monitor conversations and trends on social media, allowing them to identify sales opportunities and respond to customer inquiries in real-time. These tools can also provide valuable insights into customer preferences, interests, and behavior, which can inform sales strategies and messaging.

4: By leveraging social media and online platforms, sales teams can expand their reach, increase brand awareness, and drive sales. Social media offers a cost-effective way to reach a large audience and engage with customers on a more personal level. Additionally, online platforms such as e-commerce websites and marketplaces provide opportunities for businesses to sell their products or services directly to customers, further expanding their sales channels and revenue streams.

B: Integrating Digital Marketing with Sales

1: Digital marketing and sales are closely intertwined, and integrating the two can lead to more effective campaigns and higher sales conversions. Digital marketing plays a crucial role in generating leads and creating brand awareness, while sales teams are responsible for converting those leads into customers. By aligning digital marketing efforts with sales objectives, businesses can create a more cohesive and effective strategy.

2: Sales teams can work closely with marketing teams to align messaging, target the right audience, and create cohesive campaigns that drive both brand awareness and sales. By sharing insights and collaborating on campaigns, sales and marketing teams can ensure that their efforts are aligned and complement each other.

3: Digital marketing tactics such as email marketing, content marketing, and search engine optimization (SEO) can be used to generate leads and nurture prospects through the sales funnel. For example, email marketing campaigns can be used to send targeted messages to leads based on their behavior or interests, while content marketing can provide valuable information to educate prospects and build trust.

4: By integrating digital marketing with sales, businesses can create a seamless customer journey and increase the likelihood of converting leads into customers. By using digital marketing tactics to attract and engage prospects, sales teams can focus their efforts on closing deals and delivering a positive customer experience. This integration can lead to higher sales conversions, increased customer satisfaction, and ultimately, business growth.

C: Embracing E-commerce and Online Selling

1: E-commerce and online selling have become increasingly important in the digital age, allowing businesses to reach customers beyond their physical location. With the rise of internet and mobile technology, more consumers are turning to online channels to research and purchase products and services.

2: Sales teams can use e-commerce platforms to sell products directly to customers online, providing a convenient and efficient shopping experience. E-commerce platforms offer a range of features, such as online catalogs, secure payment gateways, and order tracking, that make it easy for customers to browse, select, and purchase products from anywhere at any time.

3: Online selling also allows businesses to track customer behavior, analyze data, and personalize the shopping experience based on customer preferences. By analyzing data such as browsing history, purchase patterns, and demographic information, businesses can tailor their offerings and marketing messages to better meet the needs and preferences of their customers.

4: By embracing e-commerce and online selling, businesses can increase their sales reach, reduce costs, and stay competitive in the digital marketplace. E-commerce allows businesses to expand their customer base beyond their local market and reach customers around the world. Additionally, online selling can help businesses reduce costs associated with traditional brick-and-mortar stores, such as rent, utilities, and staffing, allowing them to offer competitive prices and increase profitability.

Chapter 10: Global Sales Strategies

A: Expanding into International Markets

1: Expanding into international markets can provide businesses with new opportunities for growth and revenue. By entering new markets, businesses can access a larger customer base, diversify their revenue streams, and reduce their dependence on any single market.

2: Before entering a new market, businesses should conduct thorough market research to understand the local business environment, competition, and customer preferences. This may involve analyzing market trends, conducting surveys or focus groups, and gathering information from local sources.

3: Businesses should also consider factors such as regulatory requirements, cultural differences, and logistical challenges when expanding internationally. Regulatory requirements can vary significantly from country to country, so it's important for businesses to understand and comply with local laws and regulations.

4: Strategies for entering international markets may include forming partnerships with local distributors or retailers, establishing local offices or subsidiaries, or selling through online channels. Each market entry strategy has its own advantages and challenges, so businesses should carefully evaluate their options and choose the approach that best fits their goals and resources.

By expanding into international markets, businesses can access new opportunities for growth and revenue, but it's important to approach international expansion strategically and thoughtfully to ensure success.

B: Understanding Cultural Differences and Business Etiquette

1: Cultural differences can have a significant impact on business interactions and sales success in international markets. Different cultures have varying norms, values, and communication styles, which can affect how business is conducted and how sales messages are received.

2: It's important for sales teams to be aware of cultural norms, values, and communication styles in different countries. This includes understanding concepts such as hierarchy, directness, and the importance of building relationships in business interactions.

3: Understanding cultural differences can help sales teams build rapport and trust with customers, avoid misunderstandings, and adapt their sales approach to be more effective in different cultural contexts. For example, in some cultures, it may be important to spend time building a personal relationship before discussing business, while in others, business may be conducted more formally and directly.

4: Businesses can provide cultural training to their sales teams to help them navigate cultural differences and build successful relationships with customers in international markets. This training can include information about cultural norms and values, as well as tips for adapting sales techniques and communication styles to be more effective in different cultural contexts.

By understanding and respecting cultural differences, sales teams can build stronger relationships with customers, improve sales effectiveness, and ultimately, drive business success in international markets.

C: Managing Cross-Border Sales Teams

1: Managing cross-border sales teams presents unique challenges, including language barriers, time zone differences, and cultural differences. Sales managers must be mindful of these challenges and develop strategies to address them effectively.

2: Effective communication is key to managing cross-border sales teams. This may include regular meetings, clear communication channels, and the use of collaboration tools. Managers should also be sensitive to cultural differences in communication styles and adapt their approach accordingly.

3: Sales managers should provide support and guidance to their teams, ensuring that they have the resources and training they need to succeed. This may include providing language training, cultural awareness training, and access to tools and technologies that facilitate collaboration and communication.

4: Building a strong team culture and fostering a sense of teamwork can help overcome the challenges of managing cross-border sales teams. Managers should encourage collaboration, celebrate successes, and promote a sense of belonging among team members, regardless of their location.

By effectively managing cross-border sales teams, businesses can leverage the strengths and diversity of their team members to drive success in international markets.

Chapter 11: Crisis Management and Contingency Planning

A: Dealing with Economic Downturns and Market Turbulence

1: Economic downturns and market turbulence can significantly impact sales performance and revenue. During such times, consumer confidence may be low, leading to reduced spending and decreased demand for products and services.

2: To weather economic downturns, businesses should focus on preserving cash flow, reducing costs, and diversifying revenue streams. This may involve renegotiating contracts with suppliers, cutting non-essential expenses, and exploring new markets or product lines.

3: Sales teams may need to adjust their strategies to focus on selling lower-cost products or services, targeting new customer segments, or offering discounts and promotions to stimulate demand. It's important for sales teams to be flexible and creative in their approach, and to be responsive to changing customer needs and market conditions.

4: It's also important for businesses to stay informed about economic trends and market conditions, and to be prepared to adapt quickly to changing circumstances. This may involve regularly monitoring key economic indicators, such as GDP growth, unemployment rates, and consumer confidence, and adjusting sales strategies accordingly.

By taking proactive measures and staying agile, businesses can better navigate economic downturns and market turbulence, and emerge stronger on the other side.

B: Adapting Sales Strategies in Times of Crisis

1: Adapting sales strategies in times of crisis requires flexibility and creativity. Sales teams must be willing to change their approach and explore new tactics to continue generating revenue.

2: Sales teams may need to shift their focus to selling essential products or services that are in high demand during a crisis. They may also need to offer virtual sales consultations to accommodate customers who are unable or unwilling to visit physical stores.

3: Businesses can explore new sales channels, such as e-commerce or online marketplaces, to reach customers who are practicing social distancing or are unable to visit physical stores. Online sales channels can provide a convenient and safe way for customers to make purchases during a crisis.

4: By adapting their sales strategies, businesses can better meet the changing needs and preferences of customers during a crisis. This may involve offering more flexible payment options, providing discounts or promotions, or adjusting pricing strategies to reflect the current economic climate.

Overall, adapting sales strategies in times of crisis requires businesses to be proactive, innovative, and customer-focused. By staying agile and responsive, businesses can continue to drive sales and maintain customer relationships during challenging times.

C: Maintaining Resilience and Agility

1: Maintaining resilience and agility is key to successfully navigating a crisis. Businesses must be able to quickly adapt to changing circumstances and market conditions to continue operating effectively.

2: Sales teams should be prepared to pivot quickly in response to changing circumstances. This may involve shifting their focus to different products or services, adjusting pricing strategies, or finding new ways to reach customers.

3: Businesses should prioritize communication with customers, employees, and other stakeholders to maintain trust and transparency. This may involve providing regular updates on how the business is responding to the crisis, addressing concerns and questions, and soliciting feedback to improve their response efforts.

4: By maintaining resilience and agility, businesses can not only survive a crisis but also emerge stronger and more competitive in the long run. Businesses that are able to adapt quickly and effectively to changing circumstances are more likely to retain customers, attract new business, and weather future crises.

Chapter 12: Ethical Selling Practices

A: Building Trust and Integrity in Sales

1: Building trust and integrity in sales is essential for long-term success. Trust is the foundation of any successful relationship, and it is particularly important in sales, where customers are entrusting their money and needs to the salesperson.

2: Salespeople should be honest and transparent in their dealings with customers. This means providing accurate information about products or services, including their features, benefits, and limitations. It also means setting realistic expectations about what the product or service can deliver.

3: Building trust also involves following through on promises and commitments. Salespeople should do what they say they will do, whether it's following up with a customer, providing additional information, or delivering a product or service on time.

4: By building trust and integrity, salespeople can develop strong, long-lasting relationships with customers based on mutual respect and transparency. Trust leads to repeat business, referrals, and positive word-of-mouth, all of which are essential for sales success.

B: Avoiding Manipulative and Unethical Sales Tactics

1: Avoiding manipulative and unethical sales tactics is crucial for maintaining trust and credibility. Customers are more informed and empowered than ever before, and they can quickly spot sales tactics that are dishonest or deceptive.

2: Salespeople should refrain from using high-pressure sales techniques, such as creating a false sense of urgency or using misleading statements to persuade customers to make a purchase. These tactics can damage trust and credibility and ultimately harm the relationship with the customer.

3: Instead, salespeople should focus on understanding customer needs and providing solutions that genuinely benefit them. This involves listening to customers, asking questions to understand their needs and preferences, and offering products or services that meet those needs.

4: By avoiding manipulative and unethical sales tactics, salespeople can build a reputation for integrity and trustworthiness. Customers are more likely to do business with salespeople and companies that they trust, and they are more likely to recommend them to others. This can lead to increased customer loyalty, repeat business, and referrals, ultimately contributing to long-term sales success.

C: Contributing to Long-Term Customer Relationships

1: Contributing to long-term customer relationships involves more than just making a sale. It's about building a strong foundation of trust and loyalty that will keep customers coming back for repeat business.

2: Salespeople should focus on building rapport with customers. This means taking the time to get to know them, understanding their needs and preferences, and showing genuine interest in their success.

3: Providing ongoing support and assistance is also key to building long-term customer relationships. This may involve following up after a sale to ensure customer satisfaction, providing additional information or resources, or offering personalized recommendations based on the customer's needs.

4: By contributing to long-term customer relationships, salespeople can create loyal customers who are more likely to repeat purchases and recommend the business to others. These loyal customers can become valuable advocates for the business, helping to attract new customers and drive growth over time.

Conclusion: The Future of Sales Strategy

A: Embracing Innovation and Change

1: The future of sales strategy will be shaped by rapid technological advancements and changing customer behaviors. Sales teams must be proactive in embracing innovation and change to stay ahead of the competition and meet the evolving needs of customers.

2: Sales teams can embrace innovation and change by adopting new technologies such as artificial intelligence (AI), machine learning, and data analytics. These technologies can help improve sales processes, enhance customer interactions, and drive sales growth.

3: For example, AI can be used to analyze customer data and provide personalized recommendations, while machine learning can help predict customer behavior and trends. Data analytics can provide valuable insights into sales performance and help identify areas for improvement.

4: Embracing innovation and change will require a willingness to experiment, take risks, and adapt to new ways of working. Sales teams must be open to trying new approaches and learning from both successes and failures to drive continuous improvement and stay ahead in an increasingly competitive market.

B: Continuous Learning and Adaptation

1: Continuous learning and adaptation will be essential for sales teams to succeed in the future. With the pace of change in technology and customer behavior, sales professionals must stay updated on industry trends, new technologies, and best practices to remain competitive.

2: Sales professionals can stay ahead by regularly attending training programs, workshops, and conferences related to their industry. These events provide opportunities to learn from industry experts, gain new perspectives, and stay updated on the latest trends and technologies.

3: Seeking mentorship and networking opportunities can also help sales professionals learn from others' experiences and stay connected to industry trends. Mentors can provide guidance and support, while networking can lead to new business opportunities and collaborations.

4: By continuously learning and adapting, sales teams can stay ahead of the curve and drive innovation and growth. Sales professionals who embrace continuous learning are better equipped to anticipate and respond to changes in the market, ultimately leading to greater success and competitive advantage.

C: Building a Sustainable and Successful Sales Culture

1: Building a sustainable and successful sales culture will be key to attracting top talent, retaining employees, and driving long-term business success. A strong sales culture is characterized by a shared set of values, beliefs, and behaviors that guide interactions both within the sales team and with customers.

2: A strong sales culture is built on a foundation of trust, integrity, and collaboration. Sales teams must trust each other and their leaders to act with integrity and honesty in all dealings. Collaboration is essential for sharing ideas, best practices, and resources to achieve common goals.

3: Sales leaders play a crucial role in fostering a culture that values teamwork, creativity, and accountability. They should lead by example, demonstrating the behaviors and values they expect from their team members. Sales leaders should also provide support and resources to help team members succeed and hold them accountable for their performance.

4: By building a sustainable and successful sales culture, businesses can create a positive work environment where employees are motivated to achieve their best and customers are valued and respected. A strong sales culture can lead to increased employee engagement, higher productivity, and improved customer satisfaction, ultimately driving long-term business success.

www.ingramcontent.com/pod-product-compliance
Lightning Source LLC
Chambersburg PA
CBHW070348230526
45471CB00006B/2475